Unearthly Pleasures

Poems by Steve Evans

in case of emergency press

We are proud to acknowledge the Traditional Owners of country throughout Australia and to recognise their continuing connection to land, waters, and culture.

We pay our respects to their Elders past, present, and emerging.

We support recognition, reconciliation, and reparation.

Acknowledgements

In the Wreckage [*Social Alternatives*]
Back [*Social Alternatives*]
The Body Electric [*Shaping the Fractured Self*]
Conference in Japan [*APIRA Conference 2013*]
Late [*a winner in the ACT 'Poems on Walls' competition 1999*]
The Official Report [*Text*]
Piano Lesson 1: Prelude [*Artstate; Friendly Street Reader No. 30; Text*]
Poem Written Backwards [*Critical Perspectives on Accounting*]
Popular Culture [*Best Australian Poems 2015*]
Refugee Train [*Social Alternatives*]
Security [*Silver Singing Streams; shortlisted for 2015 Satura Prize*]
Setting [*The Canberra Times*]
The Sporting Life [*The Canberra Times*]
The Suburbs [*The Canberra Times*]
The Ways [*Social Alternatives*]
We Were Gold [*Divan*]

Front cover photograph, 'Cloud Dog Chasing Ball, Bellana 2017', by **Steve Evans**

Unearthly Pleasures

Steve Evans

in case of emergency press
http://www.icoe.com.au
Travancore, Victoria
Australia

Published by In Case of Emergency Press 2021

Copyright © Steve Evans 2021

All rights reserved. Without limiting the rights under copyright reserved above, no part of this publication may be reproduced, stored in or introduced into a database and retrieval system or transmitted in any form or any means (electronic, mechanical, photocopying, recording or otherwise) without the prior written permission of both the owner of copyright and the above publishers.

ISBN 978-0-6485571-7-3

His gaze is down at her,
the beautiful flesh,
and hers is up, beyond me.
I am just a passing cloud.

from 'Security'

Table of contents

Put Together	1
Popular Culture	3
Setting	5
The Future of Tennis	6
Security	7
Photographs	9
Days of Gods	10
In the Wreckage	12
Piano Lesson 1: Prelude	13
The Lake House	14
Hostages	15
Alight	16
By the River	17
My Mother Says	18
Horseshoe Bay	19
The Sporting Life	20
Back to the Studio	21
The Official Report	22
About the Author	23

Put Together

1.
I murdermouth
put together wrong

someone saw me do it
but isn't telling

I whisper at their sleep
just in case

2.
slaughtermouth me
I mist their window

I sweetspeak
charm cool as moonlight

I am careful now
more than ever was

3.
I mudmouth
licking the frost off

hear any rooflander wing
any footfall too quiet

streets they don't know
I feel, I smell

4.
before again
before twice or three

my next time
carefuller

someone saw me do it
but isn't telling yet

Popular Culture

Popular Culture came to stay.
I knew who it was, of course,
straight away.
I'd seen the photos everywhere
as we all had,
read about the drug bust and the divorce,
the horrible saga of the great weight loss,
so many gaudy headlines in supermarket queues.
She was always out there,
loud-mouthed, garrulous,
an opinion on everything.

I'm tired, she said,
and dropped her bags
right there on my step,
a stranger,
can I just rest a while?
She asked to stay a week, then two,
a month if that was okay,
then the days slowly unwound.
She stopped checking the street
every time the news showed her face.
Junk food, bare feet, late night TV,
we sat and talked Proust and Wenders
and she relaxed.

Did I sleep with her?
None of your business!
She came, she went.
I wore dark glasses.
Speak to my lawyer.

Setting

I set the fields on fire.
I go into dirt roads at night
with the only light to guide me
still snuck into my pocket,
but its flare will show
its little flash of genius,
will awaken trucks and houses,
bring flames and sirens' warm applause.

I set the fields on fire.
Bright fences strung like burning music
while cattle dumb as cattle
watch their own world turning black.
Dams exhausted, sheds ablaze,
tanks run dry as a stalled argument
while all the township's spilling out
to watch the sky gone yellow.

I set the fields on fire,
angel of the sweet dark work,
because we need to simplify,
to strip it all to basics.
I'll show you how combustible
you are in your paper boxes.
Look out your window —
that's me on fire, that's me.

The Future of Tennis

Players' clothing must feature
one bio-energy consortium logo
and a celebrity human rights endorsement.
But no Bono, thanks.

Some digital intervention
will be permitted.
Players may substitute
an avatar for up to one game each.

There will be a soundtrack
released for each main match
and a range of action figures
with motivational sayings.

The stock market will deal
in tennis futures.
Players' aces will be tradable
for carbon credits.

There must always be a racquet.
There may or may not be a net.

Security

After the ball

We're dressed like cops
but no-one gets arrested.
The usual stuff is checking locks,
patrolling parks and corridors on campus
with torch and keys, like keepers in old movies.
All the doors I pass, the handles I turn.
All the hours spent on the round,
sometimes a comforting burst
of static from the two-way
when another guard gets lonely.

Tonight the year's-end bash winds down,
the last band packs its truck
and our herding is a gentle affair.
We shuffle drunken students
into metro buses
before I take to my car
and the late-night loop begins
through this toy-town in its sleep.

When I spot the couple, naked,
sprawled on the warm asphalt
of the Vice Chancellor's parking space
and hard at it,

Unearthly Pleasures

I lean from my car window to ask
'Will you be long?'
The gasping man, politely, answers, 'No'
without turning.
His gaze is down at her,
the beautiful flesh,
and hers is up, beyond me.
I am just a passing cloud.
She is fixed on the stars
that fall into her blaze,
and I fall in there too,
just wanting now to be home in bed
with someone to watch over me.

Photographs

> *Here are the photographs taken when we were alive.*
> Carolyn Forché, *'Nocturne'*

Just one angle
where light struck a moment
and that accident of time took us,
but this is not us.
We breathed,
we swore,
we loved,
we were candid, inelegant,
lovers and liars—
though what use are we now,
curious as a crystal radio set
or a book of etiquette?

We are waiting all the same
in a box at the back of the wardrobe,
in an envelope in the bottom drawer,
or pressed between pages 12 and 13
in Borges's *Collected Fictions*,
our faces calm as strangers'
that we never knew we wore
when we were alive.

Days of Gods

I did not begin the day by thanking
the small god of the breakfast bowl,
or the one of refrigeration,
nor the one who charmed the bird
that now visits my balcony
full of dawn's unearthly pleasures.

There's no time for that.
It would be like counting grains of sand.
But I did thank the god of
the skimpy pyjamas you wore
and unwore before dawn broke.
Bless this one first of all.

There's no unemployment here —
room for any number of gods.
Millions would fit
on the head of a pin,
if the god of pins allowed.
A god of accounting, and of forgetting too.

Who are the angry gods,
the ones with unsettled childhoods
singing she-done-me-wrong songs
with bitter lyrical twists?

Got to have them too —
darker gods with dark agendas.

And what's the hierarchy?
Is there a god of gods
to whom the others defer, give thanks?
Yes, says the bird on my balcony,
but it's not you or me.
That divine one doesn't know she wears the crown.

In the Wreckage

One of the dead
has a photo in his wallet
of a woman we can't identify.
She means something
we suppose.

Another has a clipping
from a 10-year-old paper;
a creased picture and caption.
Perhaps a former lover.
We can't yet say.

Next to the old man's body
is a single pendant with
two halves of a silver moon.
His or someone else's?
So it goes.

Travellers in life, then sudden death,
collateral damage
sprawled around us in the field
as casually as sunbathers.
a tribe of broken strangers.

Piano Lesson 1: Prelude

before you play
you must empty your mind of music

Close your eyes.
Picture a plate with one cherry;
its stalk a dry umbilicus.
Picture a struck match
that fizzes but will not light.
Imagine waking in winter;
the cold floor's first touch.
Think of your mother
teaching you to tie laces,
then kick off your shoes.
Imagine sheet after sheet
of blank paper.
Now open your eyes.
Cut an orange in half
and count the spokes.
Turn your lover's photo away.
Flex your fingers.

When you have forgotten
the point of all this,
the existence of music,
open the telephone directory
and look under 'Piano Lessons'.

The Lake House

The house on the lake
is grey as the clouds,
the water like scratched tin.

The killer is in the kitchen
writing a note to his mother
who died before the war.

The bones, he writes, are honoured
with a cairn high on the hill
and a low, constant wind.

Mother, he says,
it will be fine
as soon as I work out
how to stop
all this senseless mercy.

Hostages

The other ones—
not those flashed around the world's headlines,
not those seized from schools or limousines
or found locked in farm sheds beyond the range
of road or radio or phone.

The other ones who spend the brittle hours,
the months and years,
unmissed and never ransomed;
held fast to kitchens and bedrooms
in every town and city,
sworn to years of silence.

The only politics here is thuggery,
brutally slow,
and if they ever come to the TV news,
it's as bodies in alleys
or as puzzled domestic killers
blinking at a new light
without him blocking it now.

Alight

When we caught alight,
no-one saw the blaze.
When we caught alight,
no-one offered grace or benediction.

Brighter suns have burnt—
light that glanced off windows
and fell away unseen,
universes folding into darkness,
but someone lit our fuse;
someone was the spark.

No-one saw us, though.
We were ghosts even before we died;
a swirl of dust, forgotten tunes,
songs lost on the wind.

By the River

We pretend to be angels,
going for the feel of it—
with voices like angels pretending to sing.

We pretend to be angels,
so full of ourselves—
unconvincing beasts with broken wings.

We pretend to be angels
but no one falls for it—
we are dirty, foul-mouthed, fallen things.

Oh, heavenly choir.
Oh, host of cherubim.
Don't come crying to us
when your ranks are thin.

We'll be down by the river,
pretending to be angels,
singing for one who would be king,
where we're sure that God can't see us.

My Mother Says

If you don't eat your dinner now
your father will rise from his grave
and walk this city through the rain
to lecture you on the starving in Africa,
about how he worked late shifts
all the killing factory years
to put food on this table,
and how that sound out in the street
is probably him coming here this very minute.

I sneak a peek through the kitchen curtains
and see his ghost stopping a passer-by,
maybe to ask for our address,
before shuffling off in the wrong direction,
bewildered, and probably hungry.

Horseshoe Bay

On the winter beach
a nearly full moon lights
the bony glitter of the waves' collapse.
Here the water throws itself away.
The rolling arc of its back
dissolves into white
and slides from the shore,
but always returns,
the muted plush of that roar
repeated in the numb music of its chant
like a meditation on futility.
A few around here have come late at night
and cast themselves into its dumb show
without hope of ever striking land again.

A dog barks from darkness.
I get up to leave.
Behind me the waves are a song about waves
singing nothing to do with me.

The Sporting Life

Okay, I admit it,
I was a bit of a lad.
I got caught in slips more than once;
the camera doesn't lie,
but I reckon I had you all stumped.
Just look at me,
the prodigal returns,
and I'm back in the fold
after my thousand and one nights.

You can't pin me down.
I was a book once, though I never read it.
Now I'm a ringtone and
a brand of smokes,
and soon I'll be film rights;
a blond franchise with an eye
always on the sporting life,
and then (why not?) PM.
That'll be this loveable larrikin's finest spin.
Which party? Any bloody party!

Back to the Studio

The victims were lined up here
at a quickly dug trench
before being shot,
women and children included.
Now back to the studio.

The missing girl's body was found
gagged and bound
inside a disused freezer
in the empty house next door.
Now back to the studio.

More than one hundred
refugees on the boat
that capsized in rough seas
are still unaccounted for.
Now back to the studio.

Now back to the studio.
Now back to the studio.
Now back to the studio.

The Official Report

Sometimes it goes out at two
in the morning,
moving through unlit streets
with no apparent purpose.
Whatever language it knows
is silent then too.
I have seen it motionless in the orchard,
a carpet of fallen peaches beneath
and the rain's touch light as kisses.

It scratches itself on a joke
and curls up next to misery.
It keeps looking up through
the cloud-spattered sky
at the stars
as if remembering.

Basically, it is just like
all the other aliens.

About the Author

Steve Evans previously ran and taught in the Creative Writing Program at Flinders University. He writes poetry, novels, nonfiction, and has won several major literary prizes, including a Queensland Premier's Poetry Prize and a Barbara Hanrahan Fellowship.

Steve is a reviewer, the literary editor for an international journal, and a prose editor for an Australian journal. Among his other 14 books is a history of Adelaide's Friendly Street Poets readings, Australia's longest running series of community poetry events.

He is a regular at spoken word events and has been a writer-in-residence in Australia, Singapore, New Zealand and Japan. He has also been on organising committees for seven literary festivals, and on arts funding and literary prize panels. Steve was recently part of a focus group contributing to the new South Australian Government Arts Policy.

Other Publications
Poetry
Adult Fiction
Algebra
Animal Instincts
Bonetown
Edison Doesn't Invent the Car
Luminous Fruit
Taking Shape
Useful Translations

Fiction
Easy Money and Other Stories

Edited Poetry
Another Universe (with Kate Deller-Evans)
Best of Friends: the first 30 years of the Friendly Street Poets (with Kate Deller-Evans)
Corridors: Words on the Ward (with Kate Deller-Evans)

Nonfiction
Balancing Act: The Creative Writing Pathway to Understanding Accounting (with Lee Parker)
Lift Off! an introductory course in creative writing (with Kate Deller-Evans)

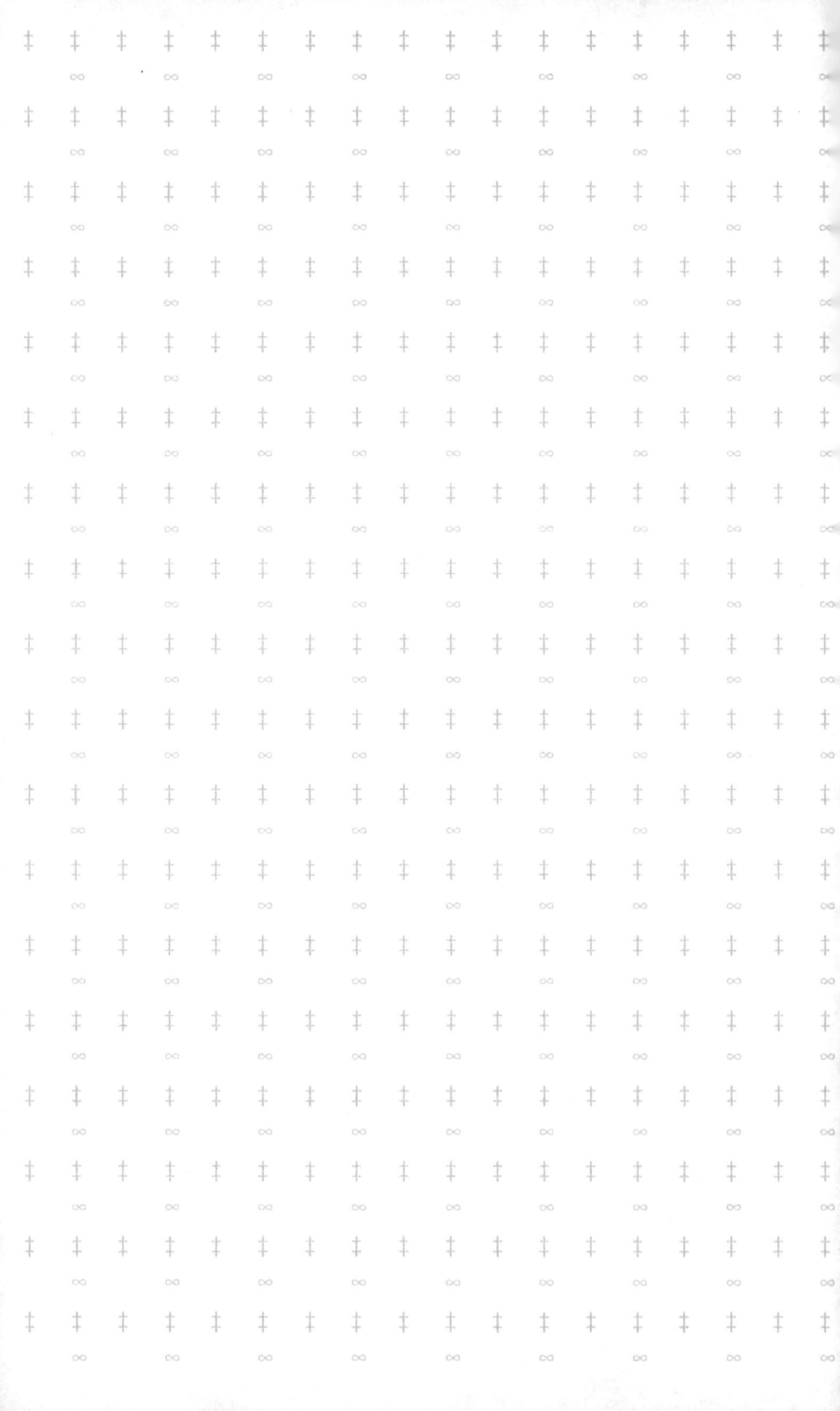

www.ingramcontent.com/pod-product-compliance
Lightning Source LLC
Chambersburg PA
CBHW020331010526
44107CB00054B/2075